Everywoman

A Verse Drama

Hugh Steadman Williams

Samuel French—London
New York — Sydney — Toronto — Hollywood

EVERYWOMAN

A verse drama based on and freely adapted from the fifteenth-century morality play *Everyman* and Hugo von Hofmannsthal's *Jedermann*

Characters

The Voice of God
Death, a terrorist
Everywoman
Everywoman's Secretary
Mafia Boss, the Devil
Widow
Crystal, Everywoman's Daughter
Nurse
Lust, Everywoman's lover
Lord Success, Company Chairman
Ambition
Money } Company Directors
Dr Know-How
Faith, Everywoman's Husband, whom she deserted

The action of the play takes place within one day

Time—the present

AUTHOR'S NOTE

The setting should be abstract, but needs to denote:

    (1) An office
    (2) A park
    (3) A boardroom
    (4) A bar
    (5) A country road

EVERYWOMAN

Music

A blinding light shines into the eyes of the audience

As the music fades a voice is heard from loudspeakers all round the auditorium and thus from no one single direction

Voice of God I am God—and I can see
All you down there who cannot yet see me.
But that will come, so never fear:
None yet may see, but all can hear.
So listen now, attention pay,
Note carefully what I have to say.

I have a problem, nothing new,
But something that affects all you.
From mankind's dawn dates this enigma:
Why mar perfection with a stigma?
For from a flaw in man's creation
Stems all the present situation:
As well as sunshine—nuclear rains;
As well as harvests—hunger pains;
While some live lives of joy and gladness,
Others suffer hurt and sadness.
And to understand is harder still
Because I gave to man free-will.
For him I did not want as slave
But son, so to him I this option gave:
To serve me freely—or himself to please—
My way—or his—to choose with ease.

And now this other puzzle scan:
Man serves me freely—or falls slave to man;
All his intelligence and all his skill
Become the instruments of self-will,
And blinded and deafened by his pride
He seeks all nature's laws to override:
With relative values, relative views,
Relative truth and relative news;
He can do anything, or so he reckons—
Until a spectre stands and beckons:

A figure dressed entirely in black, with stocking-mask over its face and holding a sawn-off shotgun in its hands, appears in silhouette

> Death—decay of flesh, collapse of bone,
> The only Absolute man will own.
> Though every law he tries to bend,
> This finite law remains—his End.

The figure of Death disappears

> But what is End for mankind sinning,
> For those who choose is the Beginning.
> For death with me is life eternal,
> Without me, emptiness infernal.
>
> And so my problem, you will see,
> Is how to reconcile to me
> Wilful man without destroying
> My own rules. It's most annoying.
>
> But that's not all, there still is worse—
> This problem really is a curse—
> For wilful man is fairly common,
> But now I have to deal with—wilful Woman.

Everywoman appears in silhouette. She is in early middle age and dressed as a smart business-person

> Take her down there, so confident, so free,
> Everywoman—how can she be turned to me?
> She's tough, ambitious, brainy, charming,
> And she's one of many who are quite alarming.
> Successful too, assuming power,
> Sure they were born for woman's hour.
> They have no time for men who them downtrod;
> Full of themselves, they have no time, either, for God.

The silhouette of Everywoman disappears

> Women need different approaches, different ploys;
> You cannot treat the girls quite like the boys—
> Or can you? That's what they demand—
> Equality with men, this they command.
> Yet this to my purposes I can suit:
> They equally must face my Absolute.
> Death! Come here, you have a task.

Death appears. A thin voice which could be male or female

Death I'm here, Boss, to do what you ask.
Voice of God Go, find Everywoman and bring her here.
    She who has nothing to fear
    From men may yet fear one
    Of sex so vague, of gender none.
    Summon her hither and we shall see
    How she accounts for her life to me.
    Choose your disguise, do what you must.
Death Sexless I am, and so impartial, just.
    Male or female, young or old,
    Makes no difference: none are bold
    When face to face with Death.
    Even in pain few wish to part with that last precious breath
    Still less when life is at its height
    And all seems promising and bright;
    That's when I most like to catch them
    And from success's very throne burst in and snatch them.
    Then terror strikes the most carefree;
    For only those who fear you, Boss, are unafraid of me.
Voice of God Go quickly Death, my messenger, do not delay;
    For Everywoman must meet you face to face this day.

Death exits

The brilliant light fades. Lights come up on Everywoman at her desk, with her Secretary

Everywoman I trust the cables to New York have gone?
Secretary And the telexes to Paris, Rome and Bonn.
    These letters are for you to sign.

The Secretary hands Everywoman a folder. Everywoman reads and signs each letter in turn

Everywoman That's clear—and that—and that one's fine.
Secretary Some people are waiting ....
Everywoman   Well, they'll have to wait,
    The meeting's at eleven, I can't be late.
    You know the Board are going to elect a
    New Chairman and Managing Director.
Secretary I heard your success is now assured.
Everywoman Thanks to hard work, it's pretty well secured.
    All the main votes around the Board are mine,
    Not one will now step out of line.

Secretary One client, a widow, has been waiting now since ten.

Everywoman looks at her watch

    After your meeting? She could come back then.
Everywoman Her folder . . .

The Secretary hands it to her

    (*Reading*) Can't pay her rent? The stupid cow.
Secretary Later?
Everywoman No, let's get it over. I'll see her now.

The Secretary exits. The Mafia Boss appears. He is smartly but rather flashily dressed, with a cigar in the corner of his mouth. His broad slouch hat conceals a neat little pair of horns

Everywoman waves him away as she hears the Secretary returning

The Mafia Boss disappears. The Secretary enters with the Widow

    Yes?
Widow My husband died six months ago. I cannot pay.
    Just give me time. I'm sure to find a way.
Everywoman Six months' arrears? What do you take us for?
Widow I'm looking for work. Just give me one month more.
Everywoman Looking for work! I bet you are!
    You've had six months—you've not looked very far!
Widow It's not that easy with four children to keep.
Everywoman Typical! Breed like rabbits—then bleat like sheep!
    I'll say it again, with utmost clarity—
    We're running a property business—not a charity.
    You'll have to quit.
Widow   Please, Madam, no . . .
    You see, there's simply nowhere else for us to go.
Everywoman That's not my problem. There are scores
    Of people waiting for flats like yours.
Widow But you're a woman . . .
Everywoman   Less of your cheek.
    I want you out of that flat this week.
Widow This week! You can't mean it. Please!
Everywoman Remember—money doesn't grow on trees.
Widow (*bitterly*) On trees, no. But from shares and stocks
    In speculative apartment blocks.
Everywoman Precisely. That's our business—and it's fair.
Widow Fair!

Everywoman If you can't afford it—then don't live there.
　　Good-day to you.
　　(*To the Secretary*) Please show her to the door,
　　And see she doesn't pester me any more.

The Secretary exits with the Widow. The Mafia Boss enters.
He speaks with a broad New York accent

Mafia Boss You played that well, baby.
Everywoman　　　　　　　　　　No, I was rough.
Mafia Boss To make out in this racket you must be tough.
Everywoman What will she do, that woman, do you think?
Mafia Boss You name it, baby—prostitution? drink?
　　She'll finish in the gutter—or round the bend.
　　Whichever way—I'll get her in the end!
　　(*He laughs*)
Everywoman You're heartless.
Mafia Boss　　　　　　　　Now, about my loan . . .
Everywoman Yes, what I bought with it—a heart of stone.
Mafia Boss Cheap at the price. Softness would be your fall.

He holds out his hand
　　Today's a pay-back day, as I recall.

Everywoman goes to the safe

Everywoman This is the tenth repayment I have made.
Mafia Boss (*laughing*) Your debt to me can never be repaid.

She hands him a large wad of banknotes

Everywoman Now leave me be—there, take your money.
Mafia Boss It's paid for all those votes today, remember, honey.
Everywoman Once I have power, then I'll be free.
Mafia Boss Free of everthing—except my power—and me!

The Mafia Boss laughs, then hears the Secretary returning, and
exits quickly. The Secretary enters

Everywoman After the meeting I'm going to entertain
　　The Directors. Lay on canapés and champagne.
　　They are sure to want to drink my health,
　　My "happiness, success and wealth".
　　And if they leave the bar a little tight,
　　They'll praise the food and say the speeches were all right.
　　Spare no expense. I must be off.

Secretary   Your car is at the door.

Everywoman starts to go, then hesitates

Everywoman Funny, I could have sworn there's one thing more.
Someone else to see me?
Secretary   Later.
Everywoman   I can't think what it is.
I suppose I'm nervous—getting in a tiz!

Everywoman starts to go, then stops again and puts her hand to her head

Secretary What's the matter?
Everywoman   I suddenly felt cold.
Am I scared? No, can't be. Or maybe growing old?
A strange sensation crept across my head,
Halfway between excitement and—yes—dread.
I must pull myself together. This won't do at all—
To be so near the peak—and frightened of a fall.
It's gone. It's nothing. I'm myself again,
Like a small child greets sunshine after rain.
Last-minute nerves! I'm only human. So
Now that I am better, I must really go.

   Everywoman exits

The Secretary busies herself about the desk

   The Mafia Boss enters

The Secretary does not see him, until she turns

Secretary Who let you in here? You are a chump,
Creeping in like that. You made me jump.
Mafia Boss She's great, eh?
Secretary   Who?
Mafia Boss   The babe. The super-chick,
The doll who makes a million extra-quick,
She's terrific. Just my type, that broad.
And now they're going to make her Chairman of the Board!
I like it! What a great career.
I've watched her climb—and helped her, with a steer.
Secretary You? Who are you? What do you mean,
Barging in here like this?
Mafia Boss (*laughing*)   You mean it's not my scene?
Now cool it, baby, you don't know who I am.

Secretary No.
Mafia Boss Well I helped your boss, see, when she was in a jam.
   So now she kind of owes me something.
Secretary   I doubt that.
Mafia Boss Don't worry, baby, just a little "tit-for-tat".
   When she was younger, see, and short of bread,
   I loaned her some, so she could get ahead—
   A divorcee, still young and bringing up a daughter.
   I gave a hand, well, because I thought I ought'a.
   And, as my friends in this great corporation
   Owed me a favour, like a little compensation,
   They found her a job, gave her the breaks she needed.
   She proved me right—look how the babe's succeeded.
   She's had the brains, the drive and the ambition.
Secretary And now you claim . . .
Mafia Boss   Just public recognition,
   That's all. It's not a great request.
   Give me my due—and she can keep the rest.
Secretary Blackmail, eh? You want a nice fat roll.
Mafia Boss I don't need money, baby, I just want control.
Secretary You devil . . .

*The Mafia Boss removes his hat, revealing his horns, and bows,
mockingly*

Mafia Boss   Clever girl. Say, you'll go far.
Secretary But not with you, now I know who you are.
Mafia Boss Think of your boss, how far she's climbed with me.
Secretary That's her affair. I'd rather I stayed free.
Mafia Boss You're cracked, you know that, baby? You're just mad
   And that's far worse than simply being bad!

   The Mafia Boss exits, laughing

*In a park, a Nurse, in dark blue uniform, is pushing an invalid chair
in which sits Crystal, about fourteen and dressed in white*

Crystal The air's so fresh this morning, Nurse, so sweet.
Nurse (*aside*) All right for her, but I've got swollen feet.
Crystal Some mornings I can almost touch the clouds, but today
   They're far too high. The wind is chasing them away.
Nurse (*aside*) You'd think she was on a country walk. But hark
   At all that traffic. It's just a city park.
Crystal The ducks come waddling along to meet me,

And daffodils lift up their golden heads to greet me.
Once more around the lake, please, Nurse.

Nurse   All right.

Crystal   No, wait!

Nurse Make up your mind, girl.

Crystal   Look, over by the gate.

Nurse Without my specs on I can't see that far.

Crystal It's driving off now, but I'm sure that was Mother's car.

Nurse No doubt it was. You know this is your mum's big day.

Crystal And mine too, Nurse. She's walking fast this way!

Everywoman enters

Hello, Mother! Look! We're over here!

Everywoman (*coldly*) No need to shout, Crystal. I can see—and
hear.

Crystal Isn't it a lovely day. See how the flowers unfold.

Everywoman Still a keen wind, though. Watch you don't catch
cold.

Crystal I'll be all right, Mum. Will you push me for a while?

Everywoman Nurse will do that, child.

Crystal   Mother, why do you never
smile?

Everywoman I'm busy, dear. I have many things on my mind.

Crystal We're going to see Daddy. He smiles and he is kind.

Everywoman He spoils you, gives you everything you ask.
I have to train you, and that's a much harder task.

Crystal I love my days with him. But Mummy, I love you too.

Everywoman I know, child, I know. Love me? Of course you do.
Now I must leave you. I have an important day.

Crystal Shall I give your love to Daddy?

An awkward silence

Well, what shall I say?

Everywoman My love? Of course dear. Now, you carry on with
Nurse.
And don't get too excited.
(*To Nurse*)   These visits make her worse
I'll have to stop them. They're too upsetting.
Her father—today of all days! I was quite forgetting.

Crystal Good luck, Mother, for your meeting. I heard
It was important, though I haven't breathed a word.
Can I tell Daddy?

Everywoman   Of course, child, not that he will care

One way or the other.

Crystal   Mother! You know that isn't fair.

Daddy cares a lot and always asks about you—how you are.

Everywoman (*to Nurse*) Yes, we'll have to end these visits,
before things go too far.

(*To Crystal*) Good-bye, child. Off you go now to your play.
And I must hurry fast this other way.

Nurse pushes Crystal off

*Everywoman starts to go off in the other direction, looking back
over her shoulder at Crystal*

Lust enters

*Everywoman runs right into Lust, who embraces her. She quickly
breaks free*

Not here, you fool.

Lust   I want to hold you tight.

Everywoman Not here, I said. Our meeting is not until tonight.

Lust (*laughing*) A time and place for everything—even Lust.

Everywoman At least let's call it "love".

Lust   All right, then, if you must.
But you know as well as I do it isn't true.
You use me and I make use of you.

Everywoman Well put my friend. You're such a modern man—
Give what you must—and take all that you can.

Lust And what of you? I'm nothing in your eyes.
Only of interest from sunset to sunrise.
But come the day, you don't even want to see me

Everywoman If you feel so bad, you're at liberty to free me.

Lust Just what I mean—so uninvolved, so cold.

Everywoman I've other things to think of.

Lust   So I'm told.

Everywoman You're coming to the meeting now, I trust?

Lust When my mistress stands for Chairperson, I must.
Let's go together.

Everywoman   Together? Are you mad?

Lust About you, a little crazy. About myself—just sad.

Everywoman Well pull yourself together, can't you, until work is
done.
Our leisure and our pleasure must be earned and won.
This morning, in the Boardroom, alone I'll stand and fight.
And I'll see you in the bedroom, lover-boy, tonight.

Lust and Everywoman exit in different directions

The Lights change to a boardroom. Around a table sit five men: Success, at the head of the table, Ambition, Money, Know-how and Lust. Everywoman is the only woman present. Success rises to speak: he is white-haired and distinguished

Success For ten years, as your Chairman, I've seen this firm expand,
From modest beginnings to the strongest in the land.
With a knighthood I was honoured, as Chairman of this Board,
And now, on my retirement, they're going to make me Lord.

"Bravo". "Hear Hear" and "Quite Right" from the others

A gratifying climax to a satisfying career.
But now it's time to hand over, in my seventieth year.

Applause from the other members of the Board

And I suppose it's fitting to close this short address
With some personal observations on the secret of success.
I'm sure you won't believe this, but none the less it's true,
The key is very simple—it's to work with all of you.

Applause

With Ambition—your aggressiveness is something I can use;
And Money has such power that with him you can't lose;
And Know-how, you can put them both to work, and work with style;
And Lust—for money, power and sex—which makes it all worthwhile.
But this would all be useless, a waste and a disgrace,
Were we not to train new leadership to rise up and take our place.

Pause

Everywoman, I have passed on my best experience to you.
I nominate you for Chairperson—it's no less than is your due.

Applause from all, except Ambition

Now, can I have a seconder for Everywoman's name?

Lust raises his hand. Others follow

Lust, you were the first that privilege to claim.
Now, to be democratic, it's only right to ask—
Are there other nominations for this great and onerous task?

Success looks round the table. No-one moves. But suddenly Ambition leaps to his feet

Ambition Everywoman has been canvassing—and that's against
     the rules.
Lust Sit down, man, be quiet.
Ambition   You're all a pack of fools.
    A woman for your Chairman? I've never heard such rot.
    And if you are all afraid of her—then I at least am not.
    I know I'm called ambitious, and out for power and pelf,
    But if no-one will propose me—then I'll nominate myself!

Uproar as Ambition sits down. Success bangs his gavel

Success Order, please! Silence! Order on the Board!
    Time is money, gentlemen, and to waste we can't afford.
    Ambition has proposed himself—a strange divisive note.
    But he too must find a seconder before I call a vote.
    Without that, our rules say, must his nomination fall—
    And we've never had a contest, as far as I recall.
    Although we hold elections and conduct them right and fair,
    We've always been unanimous when voting for the Chair.
    Now, is there anyone to second Ambition's claim to stand?

Silence from the others

    I thought not and hoped not. Now we'll proceed as planned.
Everywoman One moment, Mr Chairman, I would like to have
     a word.
Success By all means, Everywoman, I think you should be heard.
Everywoman There is a motto in your boys' schools: "Play up
     and play the game".
    In the interests of fair-play, I second Ambition's name.

Uproar again. Success bangs his gavel. They quieten down

Success I think I can say, on behalf of all the Board,
    That Everywoman's conduct is something we applaud.
    She has shown herself high-minded and fair beyond all need,
    And if you elect her to succeed me, I shall be glad indeed.

He bangs his gavel

All those in favour of Everywoman's name?

All raise a hand, except for Everywoman—and Ambition

For Ambition's?

Ambition alone raises his hand

> Shame on you, sir. Fie on you and shame!
> The result I declare is that by four votes against one
> The election is decided—and Everywoman's won!

Applause, cheers etc. Success leaves his place at the head of the table, goes to Everywoman and conducts her to the empty chair. He then takes his place among the others

Everywoman Thank you, Lord Success, and thank you one and all—

> Not to exclude Ambition, despite his nasty fall.
> Ambition, I shall need you, just as Lord Success has said,
> So let's forget this incident and drop the matter dead.

She holds out her hand to Ambition, who shakes hands. Applause from the others

> Now please don't misunderstand me, I'm not preaching Women's Lib.,
> And this is not the forum for statements wild and glib,
> But isn't it apparent, from the job I have to do,
> That I shall need those qualities that appeal to all of you?
> Ambition, Money, Know-how, Lust, and, I hope, Success
> Are the mainstay of a Chairperson—in trousers or a dress.

Laughter from the others

> Now I won't deny I'm flattered that you should vote me in,
> But let us keep the speeches short, so that celebrations can begin.

Applause

> I've arranged a little party, over luncheon, in the bar;
> And you are all invited—for champagne and caviar.

More applause

> After that, it's down to business. We'll make this office hum,
> And I look forward to working with you, for many years to come.

She sits down amid loud applause. Money rises to his feet

Money Everywoman, let me be first to say that I am most impressed

By your honesty and candour, not to mention charm and zest.

I welcome you as Chairperson, and you can rest assured

That you will find your policies financially secured.

Everywoman Money, I thank you. With your wisdom and your wealth

I know that you have guaranteed our Company's good health.

Know-how Let me add my voice to Money's, and further let me say

That my know-how is at your service, any time of day.

Everywoman Without your skill and expertise no business can servive;

So thank you, Dr Know-how, together we will thrive.

Ambition Good lady, you have been kind to me, so I'll be good to you,

And back you to the very hilt in all you aim to do.

Everywoman Ambition, let me tell you that I am well aware

I can only run things with you and without you wouldn't dare.

Lust Depend on me, dear lady, my special gifts to lend,

At work or in your leisure hours, I'll always be your friend

Everywoman We are not yet well aquainted, Lust, I very much regret,

But that must be corrected, now that we have met.

Success I can retire happy now, you have fulfilled my dream—

A brilliant successor, backed by a united team.

Everywoman You have all been more than generous with promises and praise.

I can only add, sincerely, this is my day of days.

The Lights fade, then come up on a bar

Success, Ambition, Money, Know-how, Lust and Everywoman are all there. Laughter. Dance music. The men smoke cigars. They have already drunk a good deal. The Secretary hands round canapés piled high with caviar. Everywoman takes a magnum of champagne and goes round filling up glasses

Drinks are on me—so let the champagne flow.

Success Trust Everywoman to get the best champagne I know.

Everywoman fills his glass

Everywoman Fill up your glasses—then I'll propose a toast.
Lust On the contrary! Let's all drink to our host.
All cheer and raise their glasses.

Lust and Money lift Everywoman so she is sitting on the bar, the bottle of champagne in her hand. Success starts singing, they all join in

All the Men For she's a jolly good fellow,
    For she's a jolly good fellow
    For she's a jolly good fellow—
    And so say all of us.
    And so say all of us,
    And so say all of us
    For she's a jolly good fellow . . .

At the climax of the song there is a gun-shot

   Death bursts in

The Secretary screams. Everyone freezes with fear

Death Stay where you are, everyone, keep calm,
    And no-one will come to any real harm.
    Now do just what I tell you. I've been hired
    To take your Chairman hostage.
Success   What me?
Ambition   No, you've retired.
Success (*with relief*) Ah, so I have.
Death (*moving towards Everywoman*) Come along, I know my
             quarry.
Success Hurray! I'm Chairman no longer.

He realizes. Death is looking at him

                           Awfully sorry.

Death, now beside Everywoman, points his gun at her

Death One move, and I'll empty this into her head.
    Come, Everywoman, you're as good as dead.
Everywoman Cowards! Five men, all seized with fright,
    Would let him take one—person—without a fight.
    Have you not all just pledged your loyalty to me?
Money From acts of war, or civil riot, our obligation's free.

Ambition Besides, we are so clever,
Money So wealthy,
Know-how And so skilled,
Success That we have a solemn duty not to let ourselves get
    killed.
Everywoman And Lust—you pledged your love . . .
Success What?
Lust But
    not my life.
    Besides, it's common knowledge—you're someone else's wife.
Success A scandal in the Boardroom? That's bad indeed.
    From our Chair—person—we expect a better lead.
Ambition That's why I stood against her. I always knew
    That to have a woman Chairman wouldn't do.
Money Money's what he's after, so let's not make a fuss;
    He'll get far less in ransom than if he captured one of us.
Death Fine friends you have around you, loyal and true!
Everywoman So much revealed so quickly—through fear of you.
Death That's what I discover as I travel round the earth.
Everywoman Lust, Money, Success and Know-how, now I know
    your worth.
Death Come, then, Everywoman, your education has begun;
    You'll learn much more of life and death before our journey's
    done.
Everywoman Wait, please! We cannot go so quickly.
Death Oh yes we can.
Everywoman My daughter—she is weak and sickly;
    I must make arrangements for her care.
Death If you had cared sooner, she wouldn't need that chair.
    No, it's too late, Everywoman, your chance has passed.
Everywoman A little time, I ask you.
Death Time!
Everywoman —goes by so fast.
    Time to savour the things I've pushed aside
    In my drive towards the top. All the pleasures I've denied
    Myself. Time to read, to think, to ponder,
    Time to enjoy a summer garden, time to wander,
    Time for music, painting, drama,
    Time to feast on nature's panorama:
    A rocky coastline, the dawn on alpine snow,
    A lakeside sunset or a river's silent flow;
    Time to discover, perhaps, my own creative talents . . .

Death A waste of time! Your soul hangs in the balance.
Everywoman Also, I've had such little time, in my short span,
    To worship God, or serve my fellow-man.
Death If time would help you, then I would give it;
    But would your life be any different, could you re-live it?
    I doubt it. You would still worry about power,
    Success and wealth at every wakeful hour.
    Time would profit you nothing. No, today's the day
    I must present your bill—and you must pay.

Death starts to take Everywoman away

  The Mafia Boss strolls in

Mafia Boss Hello, my my, what's this before my eyes?
    A stick-up in a Boardroom! Well, surprise, surprise!
    Everywoman, baby, is this hood bothering you?
    Leave it to Uncle, he knows what to do.
    (*To Death*) You want a hostage, right?—to raise some dough.

    (*He pulls out a wad of banknotes*)

Death There's more to this, my friend, as you well know.
Mafia Boss Cool it, pussycat, Like what's your price?
    I'll buy her from you.

    (*To Everywoman*) Now ain't I nice?

Death She comes with me, those are my orders,
    To travel far beyond these earthly borders.
Mafia Boss Orders from whom? You mean your Boss?
    I served him once, you know. The double-cross.
    A prince I was, happy as Larry,
    He did me down, made me fetch and carry;
    I couldn't stand it, quit, and started on my own.
    So you're his hit-man? I might have known.
    The broad is mine, owes everything to me.
Death From all of that my kidnap makes her free.
Mafia Boss Everywoman, honey, tell this creep the truth—
    Like how we've been partners, ever since your youth.
Everywoman Partners I'm not sure, but yes, you helped me climb.
Mafia Boss (*to Death*) So take the money and don't waste my
    time.
Everywoman But I've always felt uneasy with our arrangement.
Mafia Boss Don't listen to your conscience, baby, that brings on
    derangement.

Everywoman You wanted everything under your control.

Mafia Boss I only wanted one thing, honey—your everlasting soul.

Death That's something you've no right to ask, and she no right to give.

Everywoman And I know now I won't give it as long as I shall live

Mafia Boss That won't be long, sister, if Death takes you away. You're finished if you go with him.

Everywoman (*looking round at her colleagues*) I'm finished if I stay.

I have a feeling this is decision's hour;

I would rather anything than stay within your power,

And if that means I go with Death, I'll say "farewell";

Better to travel dangerously than stay secure in hell.

The Mafia Boss goes

Death Everywoman, my orders are one favour to bestow—

You may invite whoever you please along with you to go.

Ambition It's no good asking us, I'm sure—we haven't got the time.

Know-how My knowledge is so valuable, to leave would be a crime.

Money Some say they can't afford to live—I can't afford to die.

Success To say Success deserves to live would surely be no lie.

Lust For life I crave, for life I lust with every heated breath;

It would be a contradiction were I to go with Death.

Death (*To Everywoman*) So no-one will go with you.

Everywoman   I'm not surprised, are you?

Old experts aren't much help to me when all ahead is new.

Death And it doesn't frighten you to go with me alone?

Everywoman Alone I've struggled all these years to reach Success's throne.

Death That pride that has sustained you and carried you through all,

Could now be your worst enemy and throw you to your fall.

Everywoman Then let it. I'm not afraid of you, nor of your Boss.

Crystal bursts in, wheeling herself in her chair, followed by the Nurse.

Everywoman screams in horror

Crystal Sorry for disturbing you, I hope you won't be cross.
Nurse I beg your pardon, Madam, I simply couldn't stop her.

(*She notices the black figure with a gun*)

I say, is something wrong in here? Shall I call a copper?
Death Stay where you are. No-one leaves until we're clear away.
Crystal I'm coming with you, Mother.
Everywoman   No you're not. You stay.
Crystal But where are you going, with that awful figure?
Death Stand still, I said. My finger's on the trigger.
Everywoman We're leaving on a journey, child, where no-one else
          can go.
Crystal (*to Death*) No-one? Truly? Please, I have to know.
Death I told your mother she could take anyone she chose.
Crystal Then what about me? Can't I go?
Death   Yes, I suppose
          So child, if your mother there agrees.
Crystal If I could kneel, Mother, I'd ask you on my knees.
Everywoman I don't want you mixed up in this. There's danger.
Crystal But I can't let you go alone with that dark cruel stranger.
Everywoman You have your youth, your future, your life to live.
Crystal To help you, Mother, all that I would gladly give.
Everywoman But how could you help me? I mean, what could
          you do?
Crystal I'm sick and weak, but I have love and that I'll give to
          you.
Everywoman You are too innocent, too good to be my daughter.
          Crystal you are, clear as glass and pure as running water.
          My coldness melts before your love, my guile before your
          truth
          But worse than that, you represent and mirror my own youth:
          They will all laugh and mock at this, but none the less it's
          true,
          You remind me that once I was innocent like you.
          What happened in the years between to foul the crystal
          stream?
          That is the story of my life, now over it would seem.
          Now, as I think about you, child, my heart is filled with shame
          The more I gathered worldly strength, the weaker you
          became;
          This thought I hardly comprehend, it's terrible, but true—
          The sickness of my mind and soul, expressed itself in you.

Crystal Mother, don't plague yourself with gloomy thoughts and
    sad.
    I've brought good news—and a surprise I hope will make
    you glad.

Everywoman There's little now can gladden me or brighten up my
    way
    Since Death has come to summon me.

Crystal   I visited Dad today.
    I asked him if he'd call on you—I hope you will agree;
    Instead of meeting two by two, today we can be three.

Faith enters

Everywoman Faith! What brought you here?

Faith   Crystal did, my dear.
    She said you needed me. It was entirely her idea.

Everywoman I never said I needed you. You know I never would.

Crystal But you do need him, Mummy, he's strong and kind and
    good.

Everywoman I've done without him all these years.

Crystal   But Mummy,
    how
    On earth can you do without him now?

Faith I've waited for you, faithfully, 'til you should come again,
    And I have kept my love for you, sharpened more by pain.

Everywoman Painful it was to leave you. And I was under stress;
    But I knew if I stayed with you, I might never find success.

Faith And have you found what you were looking for, at last?

Everywoman No, I must start my search again—all my success is
    passed
    And is now as much use to me as a great pile of rubble.

Faith Crystal and I will search with you.

Everywoman   No, please do not
    trouble.

Faith If you would face the truth my dear, and swallow all your
    pride,
    You'd recognize, as I do, that my place is by your side.

Death moves Everywoman, Faith and Crystal out at gun-point

The Lights fade, then come up on a road, with a wayside Cross

*Everywoman enters, with Faith, who is pushing Crystal in her
wheel-chair, and Death*

Everywoman Now you have come with me far enough, no need
    for you to suffer.
Faith I cannot say we'll be much help, but to go alone is tougher.
Everywoman You're both ready to sacrifice yourselves for me?
    No, I will not let you, it cannot, must not be.
Faith There is an even greater love you cannot earn or merit:
    Christ offered it upon that Cross. Accept it, and inherit
    All that He promised: forgiveness, peace of heart,
    Grace, and strength to follow. All this will start
    From the moment you repent your sins and ask
    To be washed clean of all that sullies. Remove the mask
    Of sophistication, the hard outer skin that tries
    To ward off the truth with armour-plated lies.
    Simplicity is there, and innocence, waiting to appear.
    Like children we must become again in order to draw near.
Everywoman (*to Faith and Crystal*) Your faith and love have
    moved me. My heart is strangely warmed,
    And all the citadels of pride are stormed
    And broken down.

She kneels at the foot of the Cross

                Lord, accept me as I am: greedy,
    Hard, ambitious, lustful, proud, but needy;
    Wash me, forgive me, make me new,
    Train me, direct me, Lord, your will to do.

*Everywoman remains on her knees in silent prayer. Faith also
kneels, beside her. Quietly and slowly Crystal steps out of her
wheelchair and walks over to Everywoman and also kneels, on the
other side. When Everywoman gets up, Crystal gets up too and she
and Faith support Everywoman on either side*

    Crystal! You're walking! After all these years!
    (*She weeps for joy*)
Crystal Yes, Mother, I'm walking. So come now, dry your tears.
    As you were praying there flowed through me a strength
    I never knew before. I feel like walking the length
    Of earth and heaven as well.
    Mother, I'd even walk with you through hell.
Faith That you will need to do no longer.
    With Faith faithful and Crystal stronger
    To plead on her behalf, she need have nothing to fear
    From Him who loves, forgives, wipes every tear.
Everywoman I feel almost like a child again, youthful, light

Of step and free of heart, awaking out of night
Into the dawning of a new life.
Death   Come, approach
The presence of the Infinite. Without reproach
He welcomes the repentant sinner.

*The Light grows very bright. The figures of Death, Everywoman,
Faith and Crystal become silhouettes. Everywoman leaves the
others, approaches the light and kneels. Death follows, a little to
one side*

Mission completed, Boss:
Everywoman—humbled, broken, reborn at the Cross.
Voice of God Well done, my messenger. Blessed are those jolted
    awake
By your summons. But more blessed are those who make
The doing of My will, not theirs, their joyful task
When life still sweeps before them and they bask
In the sunshine of fulfilment and success.
They are the saints whom future generations bless;
For they not only save their souls from hell,
But will become remakers of the world as well.

Music

*Everywoman gets up from her knees and moves off, with Death,
Faith and Crystal*

Finally, just the brilliant Light remains, as at the beginning

I am God. And I can see
All you down there who cannot yet see me.
But that will come, so never fear;
None yet may see, but all can hear.
So listen now, attention pay
To what God says, to you, today.

Music swells, then fades. A silence before the Lights fade and

the CURTAIN *falls*

FURNITURE AND PROPERTY LIST

See Author's note.

On Stage:	Desk. *On it:* writing materials, folders
	Desk chair
	Safe. *In it:* wad of banknotes
	Wheelchair
	Boardroom table. *On it:* gavel
	6 boardroom chairs
	Bar. *On it:* plates of canapès, caviar, magnum of champagne, 6 glasses, cigars, lighters
	Roadside Cross
Off stage:	Shotgun (**Death**)
	Folders of letters and papers (**Secretary**)
Personal:	**Everywoman:** watch
	Mafia Boss: cigar

LIGHTING PLOT

Property fittings required: nil
Several settings on open stage

EFFECTS PLOT

Cue 1	As scene opens *Music; fade as* **Voice of God** *speaks*	**(Page 1)**
Cue 2	Park scene opens *Sound of traffic*	**(Page 7)**
Cue 3	At climax of "For he's a jolly good fellow" *Gun shot*	**(Page 14)**
Cue 4	**Voice of God:** ". . . remakers of the world as well" *Music*	**(Page 21)**
Cue 5	**Voice of God:** ". . . to what God says to you, today" *Music swells, then fades to silence*	**(Page 21)**

MADE AND PRINTED IN GREAT BRITAIN BY
LATIMER TREND & COMPANY LTD PLYMOUTH
MADE IN ENGLAND